Election Mania: Step-by-Step Activities to Grades 3-5 about the Levels of Government, the Voting Process, and More!

Table of Contents

Election Mania: Step-by-Step Activities to Teach Kids in Grades 3-5 about the Levels of Government, the Voting Process, and More!

Acknowledgements

AUTHOR

Priscilla H. Porter is the Director of the Porter History-Social Science Resource Room at the Palm Desert Campus of California State University San Bernardino. A former elementary school teacher, Dr. Porter is the author of numerous curriculum guides and is the senior author of *Reflections*, a Kindergarten to Grade 6 social studies textbook series published by Harcourt School Publishers @2007 and adopted by the State of California.

Teacher Contributors

Cynthia Delameter - Los Angeles Unified School District
Dr. Diane Hembacher – California State University Dominguez Hills
Janice Harbin – Little Lake City School District
Kimberly Reems – Los Angeles Unified School District
Tammie Sue Price – Desert Sands Unified School District
Karen Sanders – King's Schools, Palm Springs, California

Notes from the Author

To hear about my latest books first, sign up for my exclusive *New Release Mailing List* by sending me an email at prisporter@aol.com. The next books in my grade level-specific series for teachers of Kindergarten to Grade 5 will be released later this year. Let me know your grade level of interest.

Requesting Your Review – Reviews are very important to authors. If you've enjoy this book, please write a review of it on www.Amazon.com

Direct inquiries to: Dr. Priscilla H. Porter
Palm Desert Campus, California State University San Bernardino
37-500 Cook Street
Palm Desert, California 92211
prisporter@aol.com

Overview

Election Mania: Step-by-Step Activities to Teach Kids in Grades 3-5 about the Levels of Government, the Voting Process, and More!

Elections are big news! But do kids really know how the whole process works? These easy step-by-step activities help kids learn about the levels of government, the voting process, and more! This is the one book every teacher in Grades 3-5 should have to help their students master the common core state standards for reading/language arts as they learn about their local, state and national government and our citizen's most important decision making process - voting.

Description of the Unit

Election Mania begins with rules and laws. Students look at the governance of their family and school and then at the branches of the local community, county, state, and national government. The step-by-step election process begins in Lesson 2 as students learn about their city's government and then vote to elect city council members for their class. The city council gets to work in Lesson 3 as they have to solve a skateboard problem in the city park that brings many angry citizens to their city council meeting. This sparks ideas for a service-learning project your class many want to tackle. In Lesson 4, students analyze different jobs of government and determine which level is responsible for each job. Campaign posters, speeches, voting, and the election process bring the Executive Branch to life in Lesson 5 as students determine the qualifications to be president and elect their own class president. As the unit ends, students sort the many academic, domain-specific vocabulary words they have learned into the correct branch of government.

Focus Questions

Lesson 1: Who makes the rules and who makes the laws?
Lesson 2: What form of government does our city have? Who are our elected officials? What is the function of local government? What does the local government do?
Lesson 3: How can we help solve a problem in our community?
Lesson 4: What are the three levels of government? What does each level do?
Lesson 5: What are the qualifications to be president of the United States? What are the duties of the president? What is the election process for a president?
Lesson 6: What academic, domain-specific vocabulary words are associated with each branch of government?

Correlation to Common Core State Standards

Many of the activities in this unit support and develop the Common Core State Standards for Reading/Language Arts. The abbreviation for each standard is included below. For example, RI.3.4 relates to *Reading Standards for Informational Text, Grade 3, Standard 4*.

Reading Standards for Informational Text

Craft and Structure
RI.3.4 Determine the meaning of general academic and domain-specific words or phrases in a text relevant to a grade 3 topic or subject area (Lessons 1, 2, 4, 5, 6)

RI.4.4 Determine the meaning of general academic and domain-specific words or phrases in a text relevant to a grade 4 topic or subject area (Lessons 1, 2, 4, 5, 6)
RI.5.4 Determine the meaning of general academic and domain-specific words or phrases in a text relevant to a grade 5 topic or subject area (Lessons 1, 2, 4, 5, 6)

Range of Reading and Level of Text Complexity
RI.3.10 By the end of the year, read and comprehend informational texts, including history/social studies, at the high end of the grades 2-3 level text complexity band independently and proficiently (Lessons 1, 6).
RI.4.10 By the end of the year, read and comprehend informational texts, including history/social studies, in the grades 4-5 text complexity band proficiently, with scaffolding as needed at the high end of range (Lessons 1, 6).
RI.5.10 By the end of the year, read and comprehend informational texts, including history/social studies, at the high end of grades 4-5 text complexity band independently and proficiently (Lessons 1, 6).

Writing Standards

Text Types and Purposes
W.3.1 Write opinion pieces on topics or texts, supporting a point of view with reasons (Lessons 2, 5 speech).
W.4.1 and W.5.1 Write opinion pieces on topics or texts, supporting a point of view with reasons and information (Lessons 2, 5 speech).

Research to Build and Present Knowledge
W.3.8 Gather information from print; take brief notes and sort evidence into provided categories (Lessons 1, 2, 6).
W.4.8 Take notes, paraphrase, and categorize information (Lessons 1, 2, 6).
W.5.8 Gather relevant information from print sources; summarize or paraphrase information (Lessons 1, 2, 6).

Speaking and Listening Standards

Presentation of Knowledge and Ideas
SL 3.4.a, SL 4.4 and SL 5.4.a (Lessons 2, 3 and 5).

Language Standards

Vocabulary Acquisition and Use
L.3.6, L.4.6 and L.5.6 Acquire and use accurately grade-level appropriate general academic and domain-specific words or phrases (Lessons 1, 2, 4, 5, 6).

Teacher Note: Three Branches of Government

In 1787 leaders of the states gathered to write the Constitution - a set of principles that told how the new nation would be governed. The leaders of the states wanted a strong and fair national government. But they also wanted to protect individual freedoms and prevent the government from abusing its power. They believed they could do this by having three separate branches of government: the executive, the legislative and the judicial. This separation is described in the first three articles, or sections, of the Constitution.

4

Lesson 1: Rules and Laws

Focus Question: Who makes the rules and who makes the laws?

Activity #1 Who Makes the Rules?

Materials needed: A copy of **Who Makes the Rules?** (Handout #1.1 on page 7) displayed with a document camera, an overhead transparency or on chart paper.

Step 1: Explain to students that at home they have rules they must follow in order to be safe. Display a copy of the chart **Who Makes the Rules?** (Handout #1.1). Refer students to the column titled "Home." Ask the following questions and record student responses on the chart.

- Who makes the rules in the home?
- Who enforces the rules?
- Who determines if the rules are fair? Who punishes wrong-doers? What kinds of consequences are there for not following the rules?

	Who makes the rules?	Who enforces the rules?	Who determines if the rules are fair? Who punishes the wrongdoers?
Home	Answers will vary	Answers will vary	Answers will vary

Step 2: At school, you also have rules to follow. Discuss the rules at school. Who makes these rules? Who enforces them? Who determines if the rules are fair? Who punishes the wrong-doers? Record student's ideas on the chart, **Who Makes the Rules?** Discuss, "What are the consequences of not following a rule?"

School	Teachers, students (sometimes), principal, school board, state and Federal government.	Teachers, (student council) principal, school board	State court and federal court

Activity #2 Who Makes the Laws?

Materials needed: a copy for each student of **Who Makes the Laws?** (Handout #1.2, page 8).

Step 1: Just like we have rules at home and in our school, our community has a set of rules or laws. For example, traffic laws help people travel safely on the streets. Without traffic laws, many people might be hurt in accidents. The local government (our city) has a structure for deciding who makes the laws, who enforces the laws, and who determines whether the laws are fair. Define a *government* as the group of citizens that runs a community, a state, or a country.

The **levels of government** are the local (city or town), county, state, and the national or federal government (the United States of America). Each level has branches of government where people make the laws, enforce the laws, and determine if the laws are fair.

There are also branches of government. The three **branches of government** are the Legislative Branch (makes the laws), Executive Branch (enforces the laws), and the Judicial Branch (determines if the laws are fair and punishes the wrong-doers).

Step 2: As each branch of government is discussed, help students record the information on their copy of *Who Makes the Laws?* (Handout #1.2). It is recommended you begin with the Executive Branch. If access to the internet is available, have students locate the names and appropriate photos of the people and buildings for each branch.

Completing this chart is a bit tedious and it takes time! During the unit, you will return to the chart over and over again so it is worth the effort. Below is the suggested information to include on your chart. The State Level information is for the State of California so you need to adjust it for your state.

Branches of Government	Legislative Branch	Executive Branch	Judicial Branch
Local Level (City or Town)	Members of the **City Council**. They are elected by the citizens. The City Council meets at **City Hall**.	The **mayor** is the leader of the city's government. The mayor is appointed from the City Council or elected by the citizens of the city. Most cities have a **City Manager**. The mayor and City Manager work at **City Hall**.	**Superior Court Judges** (merged with the county court) decide whether a person has broken the law. They also decide the consequences for someone who has broken the law. Judges work at the **courthouse**.
County Level	Board of Supervisors	County Administrator	Superior Court
State Level (California)	State Legislature: <u>State Senate</u> (40 senators/ 4 year terms) <u>State Assembly</u> (80 representatives/ 2 year terms)	Governor	California Supreme Court – appointed by the governor
National (Federal) Level of the United States of America	Legislature: Congress <u>Senate</u> (100 senators–2 per state/ 6 year terms) <u>House of Representatives</u> (435 members – 53 from California/2 year terms)	President – elected every 4 years for a maximum of 2 terms	Supreme Court - appointed by the President for life.

Explain that the three branches of the government are all equal, with no one branch being more important than the other. To make laws, all three branches have to agree.

Who Makes the Rules?

	Who Makes the Rules?	Who Enforces the Rules?	Who determines if the rules are fair? Who punishes the wrongdoers?
Home			
School			

Who Makes the Laws?

Branches of Government	Legislative Branch Who Makes the Laws?	Executive Branch Who Enforces the Laws?	Judicial Branch Who determines if the laws are fair?
Local Level Government (City)			
County Level Government			
State Level Government			
National (Federal) Level Government United States of America			

Lesson 2: Local Government

Focus Questions: What form of government does our city have? Who are our elected officials? What is the function of a city government? What does the local government do?

There are two kinds of local government in California: county governments and city or town governments. This lesson focuses on city government. The website for your city will be helpful in completing the activities that follow.

Locate the following information for your area. For example, a list of the cities in the Coachella Valley of California includes: Cathedral City, Coachella, Desert Hot Springs, Indian Wells, Indio, La Quinta, Palm Desert, Palm Springs, and Rancho Mirage.

Unincorporated areas and towns include Bermuda Dunes and Thousand Palms in the west end of the valley; Indio Hills, Sky Valley, North Palm Springs and Garnet along the northern rim; and, Thermal, Valerie Jean, Vista Santa Rosa, Oasis and Mecca to the southeast.

Indian Reservations in the Coachella Valley area include The Cabazon Band of Mission Indians, Twenty-Nine Palms Band of Mission Indians, Agua Caliente Band of Mission Indians and the Torres-Martinez Tribe. Each has its own tribal government and website.

Activity # 1 Our City

Materials needed: A copy for each student of *Our City* (Handout #2.1 on page 15)

As you complete this activity, have students complete a copy of *Our City* (Handout # 2.1).

Step 1: City Incorporation. Tell students the date of incorporation for your city or have them search the city's website for the information. This incorporation date is referred to as the date the city was *chartered*. Have students predict reasons why their city chose to become an incorporated city. Refer to the teacher information below about the incorporation of a city.

Teacher Information about incorporation:
1. A community does not need to become a city. It is a choice which local residents must make.
2. All areas of the state are within a county and under its law-making authority.
3. A community may choose to gain some independence from county rule by incorporating as a municipality (city).
4. There are different reasons for becoming incorporated: to gain more control over land use, to improve services (parks, trash removal, police), and to maintain a separate identity from a neighboring city or from the county.
5. It is not an easy choice to incorporate. It can mean having to pay more for the improved local services (street maintenance, fire, police).

Step 2: City Seal. Display a copy of the city seal for your city. (Hint: Check the website for your city.) Explain that the city seal exemplifies the ideals and beliefs of our government. Discuss the different components of the seal and the meaning of each section. If time allows, compare the city seal to the county, state, and national seals (available online).

Step 3: City Motto. What is the "motto" for your community? Discuss the significance of the city motto. (i.e. "Indio: The Place to Be." Indio is also known as the" City of Festivals."

Step 4: Form of City Government. Explain to students that the city council is a group of people elected by the citizens (voters) of the city. They make laws for the city. Cities or towns have two different forms of government, the **Council - Manager** or the **Mayor-Council.**

Most cities in California have the **Council-Manager** form of government. In the council-manager form of government, voters elect a city council. The City Council chooses one of its members as mayor and they hire a city manager to help run the city. In some cities, the mayor is elected directly by the people. Display a poster size copy of the following chart.

COUNCIL MANAGER FORM OF GOVERNMENT

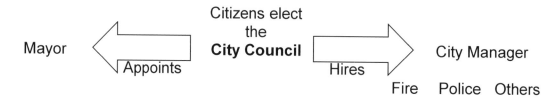

For example, the City of Indio has a Council-Manager form of government. There are five citizens elected to the City Council for terms of 4 years. The city council selects one of their members to be the mayor. A second city council member is selected to be the Mayor Pro Tem, or the next in line to become mayor.

The city council is the legislative branch of the city. The City Council
- establishes city policies
- adopts the budget for the city
- holds public hearings and listens to the people
- passes laws for the city
- hires the City Manager and City Attorney
- appoints members of city committees and commissions
- adopts ordinances and resolutions
- authorizes expenditures

The qualifications to "run" for the office of city council member are:
- resident of the city
- at least 18 years of age

The citizens also elect the **City Clerk.** The City Clerk attends City Council meetings, administers the oath of office, signs all legal documents, and takes care of the city seal, certificates, and important papers.

Activity #2 Electing a Local Government in our Classroom

Materials needed: supplies to conduct an election, i.e., ballot box, election ballots, voting booth; a class list to use for signing in at the polls.

Step 1: Citizens Vote. Ask students what they know about voting and the election process. Explain that in an election, citizens vote, the votes are counted, and the person with the most votes wins.

Step 2: Preparing for the City Council Election. Ask students what qualifications they think a city council member of our class should have. Sample qualifications are:
- a student of grade _____
- resident of room ____ for at least one month
- at least ___ years old

Develop a list of the **qualities** a city councilman should have in order to "run for office." These may include:

- honest
- smart
- hardworking

- responsible
- follows classroom rules
- listens to the ideas of others

Step 3: Nominations. To simulate an election, explain that any student who meets the qualifications may run for the City Council. Ask who would like to be a candidate. Also, ask which students would like to run for City Clerk.

Step 4: The Campaign. Candidates may select a campaign manager and make posters urging students to vote for him or her. Each of the city council candidates prepares a campaign speech telling why he/she wants the job, what his/her qualifications are, and why he/she will make a good member of the city council.

If desired, provide sentence frames to assist with speech preparation. For example:
- My name is _____
- I am running for City Council.
- I think I will make a good member of the City Council because.......

Discuss the qualities of a good campaign speech:
- maintain a clear focus
- speak clearly at an understandable pace
- be convincing

Explain to the students that they should listen to the speeches to make a decision about the candidates for whom they will vote.

Step 5: Class Election. In advance, prepare a ballot listing the full name of each candidate running for the City Council and for the City Clerk. If possible, provide an area with voting booths (study carrels). Discuss how to mark the ballot accurately with an "X."

Students should register (sign-in) at the polling place. Provide a class list and designate a place for students to sign beside their name. Students then enter the voting booth and "secretly" vote for the candidate of their choice. If desired, provide students with stickers to show they have voted.

At the designated closing time, open the ballot box and have two students open and read the ballots. Have a third student record the votes on a tally sheet. Two poll watchers observe to see that the votes are counted and recorded correctly. After the votes are counted, the recorder and watcher sign the sheet verifying the correct record of the vote.

Discuss questions about the election such as "Do you have to tell who you vote for or can you keep it a secret?" "Why might some persons want to tell and others keep it a secret?"

Alternative Selection of City Council Members Rather than having a full election process, students can work in groups (districts) to select the person they would like to be the city council representative for their group (district).

Activity # 3 City Government Description Cards

Materials needed: pencils; a copy for each pair of student of *City Government Description Cards* (Handout #2.2 on page 16). Note: Handout #2.2 on page 17 is the answer key.

Step 1: Create a vocabulary card for each job title shown on the chart below. Display the vocabulary cards in a pocket chart.

City Manager or Mayor	Police
Parks and Recreation	City Council
Fire - Rescue	City Planning
City Attorney	City Clerk
Finance	Public Works

Distribute a pencil and a copy of the *City Government Description Cards* (Handout #2.2) to each pair of students. Have students write in the job title they think fits each description.

Step 2: Conduct a *gallery walk* where students walk around the room to observe how the other pairs matched their job titles and job descriptions. Upon return to their seats, students may rearrange any of their job titles and job descriptions.

Step 3: Using a document camera or an overhead transparency, display the *City Government Description Cards* (Handout #2.2). Lead a discussion about the responsibilities of each job category.

Activity #4 The City Council Forms the Government

Materials needed: a copy of *Our Class Government* (Handout #2.3 on page 18) The City Clerk will record the names of students who will hold each job.

Step 1: Have the City Council meet to select the Mayor, the Mayor Pro Tem, and hire the City Manager and the City Attorney. The City Manager selects the Police Chief, the Fire Chief, the City Planning Manager, the Finance Director, Public Works Director, and the Parks and Recreation Director. Other departments may include Human Resources, Disaster Preparedness, Water Authority, Code Enforcement, and the Youth Advisory Council.

The City Clerk should record the names on a copy of *Our Class Government* (Handout #2.3). You may wish to determine job responsibilities for each position.

Step 2: Return to the chart completed in Lesson 1, **Who Makes the Laws (Handout #1.2)** Look at the City level of government. Using the City Government Description Cards, have students place the Description Cards in their proper branch of government. Discuss the duties and responsibilities of each position. If you have not already done so, add the names of the key people who fill these positions in your community.

Optional Activities for Local Government

The City Council Makes the Classroom Rules Explain to students that the city council members will introduce "bills" and make the laws (rules) of the classroom. (Note: It is best to keep the laws focused on the classroom because you will have control over enforcement of the laws. Avoid laws for the playground and lunchroom. If you have established classroom rules that you do not wish to change, you may select one specific topic for the new laws. Examples include the use of the classroom library; completion of class assignments and homework; use of the class computer or centers in the classroom, housekeeping rules, etc.)

First, have students meet with the city council representative of their group to brainstorm some ideas for a "law" to create a new class law (rule). The representative for each group should write down the proposed bill. During this time, it is recommended that the teacher rotate around to the groups to review their proposed bills and help students word their bills in a positive format, such as "Walk in the classroom" rather than the negative "Don't run in the classroom."

Once the proposed laws have been reviewed, hold a City Council meeting to discuss the proposed laws. Members of the class can sit in the "gallery" while the laws are presented and debated on the "floor" of the City Council Chambers. "Citizens" of the class may come forward and address the city council regarding any of the laws. Each "citizen" must state his/her name and is limited to 2 minutes. After arguments for each law have been heard, the members of City Council vote on each bill.

City Council Guest Speaker Invite a local City Council person or the mayor to visit the classroom to talk about his/her position within the local government. Formulate appropriate questions to ask such as:
1. What is your job? How did you get your position?
2. What are the qualifications for a person with this position?
3. What laws or rules do you help make?
4. How does your job affect the community?
5. What can we do to make our community a better place?

Roles of Citizens What is a citizen? Write the word *citizen* on the board. Explain that being a citizen of a democracy means you have certain *rights*. One is the right to vote. Another is the right to speak freely and share your thoughts with other people. The *Bill of Rights* of the Constitution lists the rights of all citizens of the United States.

In a democracy, citizens also have *responsibilities*. For example, the right to vote is a responsibility. The right to serve on a jury is also a responsibility. If you care about the way your country or town is governed, you have a responsibility to vote. Citizens must obey the laws of the land. They must pay taxes. They must serve in the armed forces, if needed. They must also respect the rights of others.

Scavenger Hunt Take your class on a "city walk" scavenger hunt in the neighborhood around your school. Have students look for and log examples of local government services.

City Council Meeting Agenda Check the city or county website or contact the clerk for a copy of the agenda for next meeting. Ask the clerk for a copy of the agenda for the very first city council meeting after the city was incorporated. Have your students analyze the items on the agenda. Compare these with the agenda of a current city council meeting.

City Council Meeting Take your class or interested students to a City Council meeting. In advance, reproduce the agenda and brief the students on the agenda items. Many communities broadcast their city council meetings. Videotape the meeting for replay in the classroom for analysis and for those students who were unable to attend.

Our City in 2025 Provide students with information from the planning department on anticipated changes in the community. Encourage students to create "alternative future" scenarios for your community, e.g., "Our City in 2025." Discuss what groups in the community would need to be involved for these changes to occur.

Fire Protection Invite a fire fighter to your class to share information about their services.

Laws in Our Government Explain to students that one job of government is to make laws. Ask students, "What are some laws you have to follow as kids?" Brainstorm some laws and discuss why these laws were made. What would happen if these laws did not exist? Examples might include:
- Must wear helmets when riding bikes or skates
- Cannot drive until age sixteen
- Must wear your seatbelt in a moving automobile
- Littering is prohibited
- Cannot drive faster than the speed limit
- Children must go to school
- All dogs must have a license

Our City of _____

City Name:_____

The incorporation date for our city: _____

How our city got its name: _____

_____

Three objects found on the city seal:

_____

_____

_____

City Motto:_____

Form of Local Government: _____

Mayor's Name:_____

Number of City Council members:_____

City Clerk's Name_____

Name:_____Date:_____

City Government Description Cards

Directions: Match the appropriate job with its description on the City Government Description Cards below. Use the following job titles: City Manager, Police, Parks and Recreation, Fire - Rescue, City Council, City Planning, City Attorney, City Clerk, Finance, Public Works.

  • Protects people and property • Teaches people how to be safe	 • Puts out fires • Gives first aid • Makes sure buildings are safe from fires
  • Helps city council understand the laws • Helps city solve problems about laws	 • Attends City Council meetings • Administers the oath of office • Signs all legal documents • Takes care of the city seal, certificates, and important papers.
  • In charge of running the city on a daily basis • Organizes work people do • Makes sure people are following the rules	 • Establishes city policy • Adopts the budget for the city • Holds public hearings and listens to the people • Passes laws for the city • Appoints the City Manager, City Attorney, and members of City Committees
  • Makes plans for new buildings and parks • Makes sure buildings and houses are safe	 • Takes care of cleaning water and sewers • Works on building streets and putting up traffic signs
  • Builds parks • Organizes sports and other programs for community	 • Keeps track of the city's money • Spends city's money

City Government Description Cards

Police	Fire - Rescue
• Protects people and property • Teaches people how to be safe	• Puts out fires • Gives first aid • Makes sure buildings are safe from fires
City Attorney	**City Clerk**
• Helps city council understand the laws • Helps city solve problems about laws	• Attends City Council meetings • Administers the oath of office • Signs all legal documents • Takes care of the city seal, certificates, and important papers.
City Manager	**City Council**
• In charge of running the city on a daily basis • Organizes work people do • Makes sure people are following the rules	• Establishes city policy • Adopts the budget for the city • Holds public hearings and listens to the people • Passes laws for the city • Appoints the City Manager, City Attorney, and members of City Committees
City Planning	**Public Works**
• Makes plans for new buildings and parks • Makes sure buildings and houses are safe	• Takes care of cleaning water and sewers • Works on building streets and putting up traffic signs
Parks and Recreation	**Finance**
• Builds parks • Organizes sports and other programs for community	• Keeps track of the city's money • Spends city's money

Our Class Government

Mayor _____

Mayor Pro Tem _____

City Council Member _____

City Council Member _____

City Council Member _____

City Clerk _____

City Manager _____

City Attorney _____

Police Chief _____

Fire Chief _____

City Planning Manager _____

Finance Director _____

Public Works Director _____

Parks and Recreation Director _____

Lesson 3: A Neighborhood Problem

Focus Question: **How can we help solve a problem in our community?**

Materials needed: A copy for each student of **Problem Planning Sheet** (Handout #3.1 on page 22) and **A Neighborhood Problem** (Handout #3.2 on page 23).

Activity # 1 Simulation: *A Neighborhood Problem* *

Step 1: Inform students that many laws and rules are passed because interested citizens and groups become involved. Introduce the simulation prompt:

> A park has just been built in your city. The park has new play equipment, picnic benches, a bike trail, and new basketball courts. The kids of the neighborhood are all excited! However, the city council has decided to put up a sign that says "NO SKATEBOARDING ALLOWED!" A meeting will be held on Wednesday night about the sign. Your group will present at the meeting.

Step 2: Display a copy of the *Problem Planning Sheet* (Handout #3.1). Using the simulation prompt listed above, work with students to complete the planning sheet.

Step 3: If you have not already selected city council members for your class, designate students to be members of the city council. (The size of the city council varies in different communities. Five members are common, or use the number from your community's city council.)

Distribute a copy of *Neighborhood Problem* (Handout #3.2) to each student. Assign the students who are not on the City Council to one of the six representative groups listed on Handout #3.2.

Explain to the students that they are to pretend that they are members of the assigned group and ask them to come up with arguments to support their position toward the Skateboard Park.

If possible, hold the following meeting of your City Council in the City Hall Chambers of your City Hall. Ask the City Clerk to help you follow the proper procedure for your city council meeting.

Step 4: At a City Council meeting, each group presents their arguments to the City Council.

Step 5: The City Council votes whether they will allow skateboarding at the park.

Lead a discussion with the students about the influence each group had on the decision. Ask students, "Why is civic participation an important aspect of local government?"

*The source for this simulation is unknown. Please contact me at prisporter@aol.com if you know the original source so the proper credit can be given.

Activity # 2 How Can We Solve a Problem at Our School or in Our Community? A Service Learning Project

> Materials needed: a copy for each group of *Problem Planning Sheet* (Handout #3.1 on page 22).

Step 1: Brainstorm a list of ideas for each of the following questions: What are some problems that need to be solved at our school or in our community? How might we participate in a service learning project to solve a local school or community problem? Some examples of service learning projects may include:

- **Historic Landmark** Adopt an historic landmark in your community that needs restoration.

- **Pick-Up Patrol** Beautify your school or community by cleaning-up trash or by creating a "pick-up patrol" for your school or community; write public service announcements to encourage people to keep the area litter-free; send copies to the local newspaper, radio, and television stations.

- **Harvesting for Hunger** Begin a program by planting, tending and harvesting food for a local food bank; locate a large plot of land, collect gardening materials, invite a horticulturist to talk with your students about preparing soil, germinating seeds, transplanting seedlings, fertilizing, watering, weeding, and composting; select a crop to grow that can best be used by a local food bank; divide the class into teams to determine responsibilities.

- **Recycling Program** Create a recycling program and donate the proceeds to a local charity.

- **Water Conservation** Create a water conservation checklist with two columns on the checklist – label one "try" and the other "did." Have students follow the plan for one month.

- **Homeless Shelter** Collect shoes or eyeglasses or other items for a local homeless shelter.

- **Help Others** Volunteer to help at a local preschool, day care center, or senior center.

- **Tutor** Help adult immigrants with the English language.

- **Elderly Assistance** Provide support to an elderly person or couple who needs assistance with routine and special activities.

- **Adopt a police officer or fireman** in your community; write letters to him or her; arrange for him/her to visit your classroom or for a class trip to the station; make a list of the department's needs (specific equipment, more fire fighters or policemen) and create an action plan to raise funds for the project.

- **Care Packages** Create care packages for American troops who are stationed in war zones; ask other students, family members, community members and local businesses for donations; establish military pen pals.

- **School or Community Library** To encourage use of the school or community library, have students write literary reviews of books they have read and post them in the library to encourage other kids to read; once a month, have students care for, clean, and alphabetize their shelves; paint characters from their favorite books and hang them in the children's section of the public library; volunteer to read to students in younger classes.

- **Pet Food Campaign** Organize a pet food canned drive for cats and dogs; donate the food to a local pet shelter; make posters to encourage people to adopt rescue pets.

- **Book Drive** Conduct a book drive and donate the books collected to a homeless shelter.

- **Penny Collecting Campaign** Raise money through a penny collecting campaign to raise money to plant one or more trees at the school or in the local community; include a plaque to recognize the donors.

- Develop a **"Welcome to Our Community"** kit or a **"Welcome to Our School"** kit that includes interesting facts and information about people and events important to students or adults new to the area.

Step 2: Have the students in each group select a service learning project they would like the class to undertake that will make their school or community a better place to live.

To each group, distribute a copy of the *Neighborhood Problem Planning Sheet* (Handout #3.1). Have students in each group select one of the service learning projects and complete the planning sheet with their group.

Step 3: Have students in each group propose their service learning project idea to the class mayor and city council. Have the students in the group pretend that they are members of a special-interest group and ask them to come up with arguments to support their position.

After each group presents their arguments to the members of the class City Council, the council should vote to select one service learning project based on the arguments presented by each group.

Step 4: Once the service learning project has been determined, elicit ideas from the total class and complete a Neighborhood Problem Planning Sheet (Handout #3.1) for the service learning project. Complete the project, and evaluate the results.

Neighborhood Problem Planning Sheet

A. What is the Problem?

B. Why is it a problem?

C. Who is responsible?

D. What are some possible solutions to the problem?

Neighborhood Problem

A park has just been built in your city. The park has new play equipment, picnic benches, a bike trail, and new basketball courts. The kids of the neighborhood are all excited! However, the city council has decided to put up a sign that says NO SKATEBOARDING ALLOWED! A meeting will be held on Tuesday night about the sign. Your group will present at the meeting.

SKATEBOARD ASSOCIATION:
Position: You want the sign taken down. You think you should be able to skateboard in the park because it is a public place.

PARENT'S GROUPS:
Position: You have small children that play in the park. You are afraid that a skateboarder might run over your small children.

YOUTH GROUP:
Position: There aren't many things for teenagers to do in your neighborhood. Skateboarding is good exercise and the park is a safe place to skate.

POLICE ASSOCIATION:
Position: Almost every day they must go to the park because someone is complaining about the skateboarders being dangerous.

MR. GRUMP:
Position: He is mad because skateboards are too loud and he can't take his afternoon nap. He wants to get rid of them.

MR. DORIGHT:
Position: He thinks it's wonderful to see youngsters enjoying the fresh air and sunshine. He wants everyone to stop picking on the skateboarders.

CITY COUNCIL:
Must listen to all the arguments and then make a decision.

Lesson 4: Levels of Government

Focus Question: What are the three levels of government? What does each level do?

Activity # 1 Levels of Government

<u>Materials needed</u>: For each group of 3-4 students <u>and</u> for each individual student, a copy of **Levels of Government Sort Cards** (Handout #4.1 on pages 25-26); scissors; glue; 12" x 18" sheets of construction paper for each group <u>and</u> each student.

Step 1: Provide each group of 3-4 students a set of **Levels of Government Sort Cards** (Handout # 4.1) and a sheet of construction paper. Fold the sheet of construction paper vertically into thirds and label each section National Level, State Level or Local Level. Have each group cut and sort the cards into three categories. **Note:** Some of the categories overlap and may vary according to your community. For example, "Builds and Maintain Prisons" is listed as a state level function but may be categorized as "Federal" if there is a federal prison in your area. A suggested answer key follows:

National Level	State Level	Local Level
Makes laws for the nation	Makes laws for the state	Makes laws for counties, cities and towns
Prints and coins money	Builds and maintains prisons	Provides roads, parks, hospitals
Runs the armed forces and provides national defense	Meets in the state capitol	Provides law enforcement, fire protection
Deals with other nations	Issues drivers licenses	Meets at City Hall
Meets in Washington D.C.	Governor	Mayor
President		

Step 2: Conduct a gallery walk where students walk around the room to observe how the other groups sorted their cards. Upon return to their seats, students may rearrange any of their cards. Discuss the similarities and differences of the various classification systems.

Step 3: Using a document camera or an overhead transparency, display the **Levels of Government Sort Cards** (Handout # 4.1). Lead a discussion about the responsibilities of each level. Begin with the national level. Ask, "What does the national level government do that no one else does?" Continue with each separate level of government. Place each card on a 3-column table with one column for each level of government. Help students compare and contrast the similarities and differences of the responsibilities of each level of government.

Step 4: Return to the chart, **Rules and Laws** (Handout #1.2). Discuss where each of the Governt Sort Cards fits on the chart.

Step 5: **Levels of Government Sort Cards** (Handout # 4.1).
As an assessment, have individual students cut, sort and glue the cards onto a sheet of construction paper folded vertically into thirds and labeled with the name of each level of government.

Levels of Government Sort Cards

Meets in the state capitol	Meets in Washington D.C.
Meets at City Hall	President
Provides roads, parks, water, hospitals	Runs the armed forces and provides national defense
Issues drivers licenses	Provides law enforcement, fire protection

Governor	Mayor
Builds and maintains prisons	Makes laws for the nation
Makes laws for the state	Makes laws for counties, cities and towns
Prints and coins money	Deals with other nations

Lessons 5: The President

Focus Question: What are the qualifications to be a president of the United States? What are the duties of the president? What is the election process for a president?

Activity # 1 Presidential Quiz

Materials needed: for each student, a copy of **Presidential Quiz** Handout #5.1 on page 31).

Before any discussion of the presidency, have each student complete a copy of *Presidential Quiz* (Handout #5.1). Collect the papers and do not discuss them at this time. The quiz will be reviewed again at the end of the lesson when students can revise any of their answers.

Activity # 2 Responsibilities of the President of the United States

Step 1: Review the "Executive" branch of the United States Government on the chart, **Rules and Laws** (Handout #1.2). Explain that the president is elected by the citizens of the United States through the Electoral College. Ask a variety of questions about the presidency to determine the student's prior knowledge. Examples include:
* Who is the current president?
* How does a person become president?
* What does a president do?

Step 2: Article II Section 1 of the *U. S. Constitution* http://constitutionus.com/
Briefly examine the executive office as set forth in the Article II of the *U. S. Constitution*. Discuss with students the duties of the President. In a class discussion evaluate the criteria established in the Constitution. Use questions such as:
* What are the qualifications for President established by the Constitution?
    at least 35 years old
    a natural born citizen of the United States
    a resident within the United States for at least fourteen years
* Why do you think the Framers of the Constitution included these qualifications?

Step 3: Responsibilities of the President of the United States.
Explain to students that the president of the United States is elected every four years. The president is allowed to serve only two four-year terms. Refer to Article II of the *U. S. Constitution*. Make a list of the responsibilities of the President of the United States.

Step 4: Show students a photograph of the White House. It is helpful to also have a picture of the President of the United States, the presidential seal, and a copy of the Presidential Oath of office. http://www.whitehouse.gov/kids/ (The White House)

Activity #3 Selecting a Class President

Step 1: Review the qualifications to become a President of the United States. Ask students what qualifications they think a president of their class should have. Sample qualifications:
* a student of Grade _____
* at least _____ years old

Brainstorm a list of **qualities** of a good leader. These may include:

- honest
- smart
- hardworking
- responsible
- follows classroom rules

Review the **responsibilities** of the U.S. President. Create a list of duties for your President.

Step 2 Nominations: To simulate a primary election, explain that any student who meets the qualifications may run for Class President. Ask who would like to be a candidate. Type up a ballot with all interested names and have the students vote. Select the top three to be the final candidates.

Step 3 The Campaign: Candidates may select a campaign manager and make posters urging students to vote for him or her. Each of the three presidential candidates prepares a campaign speech telling why he/she wants the job, what his/her qualifications are, and why he/she will make a good class president. If desired, provide sentence frames to assist with speech preparation:

- My name is _____
- I am running for Class President.
- I think I will make a good Class President because…

Discuss the qualities of a good campaign speech.
- speak clearly at an understandable pace
- maintain a clear focus
- be convincing

Activity # 4 Class Election

Materials needed: supplies to conduct an election, i.e., ballot box, election ballots, voting booth; a class list to use for signing in at the polls.

Step 1: Students deliver campaign speeches for Class President. Explain to the students that they should listen to the speeches to make a decision about which candidate to vote for.

Step 2: Conduct an election for the Class President. If possible, provide an area in the classroom with voting booths (study carrels). In advance, prepare a ballot listing the full name of each candidate. Discuss how to accurately mark the ballot with an "X".

Students should register (sign-in) at the polling place. Designate a place for students to sign beside their name. Students then enter the voting booth and "secretly" vote for the candidate of their choice. If desired, provide students with stickers to show that they have voted. At the designated closing time, open the ballot box and have two students open and read the ballots. Have a third student record the votes on a tally sheet. Two poll watchers observe to see that the votes are counted and recorded correctly. After the votes are counted, the recorder and watcher signs the sheet verifying the correct record of the vote.

Discuss questions about the election such as:
- Do you have to tell who you vote for or can you keep it a secret?
- Why might some persons want to tell and others keep it a secret?

Step 3: The Oath of Office
The President of the United States takes the following oath when inaugurated. Adapt the oath for your class president. Refer to Article II, Section 1 (8)

> "I do solemnly swear that I will faithfully execute the office of President of the United States, and will to the best of my ability, preserve, protect and defend the Constitution of the United States."

Step 4: Inauguration
Plan an inauguration ceremony for the new Class President. Include a swearing in ceremony and an oath of office. Accompany the swearing in ceremony with the music *Hail to the Chief*.

Step 5: Compare and Contrast
Have students help organize information into a table to compare your Class President and the President of the United States.

	Our Class President	**President of the United States**
Name:		
Residence:		
Qualifications:		
Duties:		

Ask students questions to help them interpret information in the table. Compare and contrast the Class President and the President of the United States. If desired, let students design a presidential seal for your class president.

Step 6 Presidential Signature
Explain to students the signature of a president has great importance. When the Congress sends the president a bill, it becomes law when the president signs it.

If the president is against the bill, he may choose to **veto** the bill. In this case, the bill is sent back to the Congress who can override the veto with a yes vote of two thirds of all the members. If there are not enough votes to override the veto, the bill dies.

Sometimes a President decides to do nothing: to neither sign nor veto a bill. In this case, the bill becomes law after ten days without his signature.

The president also signs proclamations. One of the most famous is Lincoln's *Emancipation Proclamation* that freed the slaves in the Confederate states. The president also signs treaties, or agreements, between countries.

Step 7: Practice Your Signature
Explain to students, "If you should become president, you will need to sign many important papers. Try writing your signature five or six ways and select the one you prefer. Practice your signature so you will be prepared."

Optional Activity: The President's Cabinet If desired, the class president may select cabinet members to assist and advise him or her. Work together as a class to determine the names of the cabinet position, such as "Secretary of Transportation." Organize all of the classroom jobs under these cabinet positions. When you, as the teacher, see that a job has not been completed, go to the cabinet member responsible for that position and request an inquiry. (They become the "nag," and not you!)

Activity #5 Who is Qualified for the Presidency? *

> Materials needed: for each student, a copy of Handout #5.2 on page 32.

OVERVIEW: This activity asks groups of students to select one of eight candidates who they feel is best qualified to be president of the United States.

Step 1: Introduction to the Activity.
Review the types of qualifications the president must have as listed above in Activity #2. Ask students if they think there should be any additional qualifications (beyond those established in the Constitution) that they think a president of the United States should possess. Should presidents, for example, have college degrees? Or prior political experiences? Have the students create a list of additional qualifications.

If the Constitution were being re-drafted today, do you suppose the framers would change any of the original qualifications?

Step 2: Selection of Candidates
The individuals listed on Handout #5.2 provide some basic biographical data about people who have been or are still active in American life. For this activity, their name and sex have been omitted. All of them however have met the three constitutional requirements for the presidency.

Form groups of at least 4 students. Provide each student with a copy of Handout #5.2.

Explain to students: You are to determine which of these eight <u>individuals</u> you think would be <u>best qualified</u> to serve as president of the United States? Whom do you feel would be <u>least qualified</u>? Let each group decide their choices.

As students complete this task, chart their decisions on chart paper or the whiteboard under "best qualified" and "least qualified." Have each group explain the rationale for their choices.

Step 3: Summarizing Questions
1. To what extent did your choices reflect the qualifications you listed in Step 1?
2. Would you modify your original list in any way?
3. Should any of the following factors be considered in selecting a presidential candidate?

Age	Previous occupation
Religion	Personal appearance
Sex	Educational background
Personality	Ethnic background
Marital status	Number of children

   Should other factors be considered, e.g. mental health? A police record?
4. What qualifications do you feel are the <u>most</u> important?
5. What qualifications do you feel are the <u>least</u> important?

*The source for this simulation is unknown. Please contact me at prisporter@aol.com if you know the original source so the proper credit can be given.

Activity #6 Presidential Quiz
Distribute the student's original copy of the Presidential Quiz (Handout #5.1) for them to review and make any revisions.

Presidential Quiz

How much do you know about being the President of the United States? Decide if the following statements are "True" (Yes) or "False" (No).

	Yes	**No**
1. The President must be a man.	____	____
2. The President must be at least 35 years old.	____	____
3. The President must be married.	____	____
4. Only a person who is a citizen at birth can be elected President of the United States.	____	____
5. The President must have military experience.	____	____
6. A person can be elected President only twice.	____	____
7. The President must earn more money than anyone else in the country.	____	____
8. The President must be a lawyer.	____	____
9. The President must obey the law, just like everyone else.	____	____

Name_____

Card 1 COLLEGES ATTENDED: Harvard University. Columbia University RELIGION: Protestant CAREER (MAJOR OCCUPATIONS): Farmer, Lawyer, State Senator, Assistant Secretary of Navy, Governor, Vice-President Candidate MARRIED: 27 yrs. CHILDREN: 6 AGE: 50	**Card 2** COLLEGES ATTENDED: None RELIGION: Protestant CAREER (MAJOR OCCUPATIONS): Investor. Druggist. Bookseller. Brigadier General in U.S. Army MARRIED: 1st spouse: 5 years until spouse's death 2nd spouse: 1 year CHILDREN: 3 by first marriage AGE: 38
Card 3 COLLEGES ATTENDED: Morehouse College, A.B. and L.H.D.; Crozer Theological Seminary, B.D.; University of Pennsylvania, Boston University, Ph.D., D.D.; Harvard University, L.L.D.; Central State College; Morgan State College RELIGION: Protestant CAREER (MAJOR OCCUPATIONS): Protestant minister; Teacher of Philosophy at Harvard; President of a Civil Rights Organization. 1 of 10 outstanding men for the year according to *Time* magazine. Nobel Prize Winner. Noted public speaker. MARRIED: 15 yrs. CHILDREN: 4 AGE: 37	**Card 4** COLLEGES ATTENDED: None RELIGION: No specific denomination CAREER (MAJOR OCCUPATIONS): Land speculator and farmer. Lawyer. Member of U.S. House of Representatives. U.S. Senator. U.S. Judge. Commander of U.S. Armed Forces MARRIED: 38 yrs. CHILDREN: none AGE: 62
Card 5 COLLEGES ATTENDED: Columbia University RELIGION: No specific denomination CAREER (MAJOR OCCUPATIONS): Writer. Served as Lieutenant Colonel in Army. Lawyer. Member of a congress. Member of a constitutional convention. Secretary of the Treasury MARRIED: 24 yrs. CHILDREN: 8 AGE: 47	**Card 6** COLLEGES ATTENDED: None (Private secondary schooling in England) RELIGION: Protestant CAREER (MAJOR OCCUPATIONS): Teacher. Journalist. Member of labor union (trade union league). United States delegate to the United Nations. Chairman of the United Nations Commission on Human Rights. Endorsed by a President for the Nobel Peace Prize. MARRIED: 27 yrs. CHILDREN: 6 AGE: 65
Card 7 COLLEGES ATTENDED: University of Alabama RELIGION: Protestant CAREER (MAJOR OCCUPATIONS): Lawyer. State Assistant Attorney General. State legislator. U.S. Judge. State Governor. Party candidate for Presidency. Served in U.S. Air Force. Noted public speaker. MARRIED: 1st spouse 26 years until spouse's death 2nd spouse: 3 yrs. CHILDREN: 4 by first marriage AGE: 55	**Card 8** COLLEGES ATTENDED: None RELIGION: No specific denomination CAREER (MAJOR OCCUPATIONS): Postmaster. Lawyer. U.S. Representative. Store Owner. State Congressman. Served as Captain in U.S. Army. Noted public speaker. MARRIED: 19 yrs. CHILDREN: 4 AGE: 51

Lesson 6: Sort the Branches

Focus Question: What academic content, domain-specific vocabulary words are associated with each branch of government?

Activity # 1 Vocabulary Cut and Sort

Materials needed: A copy for each student of *Academic Content, Domain-Specific Vocabulary Words to Cut and Sort* (Handout #6.1 on page 34) and *Branches of the United States Government* (Handout #6.2 on page 35); scissors, glue. Optional: 2 sheets of unlined paper to make a FLIP book.

Step 1: Create academic content, domain-specific vocabulary cards using the words on Handout #6.1. Have students organize the vocabulary cards on a pocket chart under the proper category: the Executive Branch, the Legislative Branch, and the Judicial Branch.

Step 2: Distribute to each student a copy of the *Academic Content, Domain-Specific Vocabulary Words for the Branches of Government* (Handout #6.1). Have students cut apart the vocabulary words and practice sorting them into the three branches of the United States government.

Step 3: Distribute a copy of *Branches of the United States Government* (Handout #6.2) to each student. Have student glue the vocabulary words under the proper category of the Executive Branch, the Legislative Branch, and the Judicial Branch.

Optional Format: Make a Layered FLIP Book

1. Provide each student with 2 sheets of paper to make a Layered Book.
2. Stack the 2 sheets of paper so that the back is one inch higher than the front sheet.
3. Fold up the bottom edges of the paper to form four tabs. Align the edges so all layers are the same distance apart.
4. Crease the paper and staple them along the top fold.
5. Label the cover "Branches of Government" and each of the tabs Legislative Branch, Executive Branch, and Judicial Branch.
6. On each tab, glue the words that relate to the branch of government.

Academic Content, Domain-Specific Vocabulary Words to Cut and Sort

Legislative Branch	Executive Branch	Judicial Branch
President	Senate	Supreme Court
White House	Capitol Hill	Justices
Inauguration	Congress	Chief Justice
Speaker of the House	House of Representatives	Commander-in-Chief
uphold a law	Majority Leader	the "High Court"
Veto	Bill	the "bench"
Chief Executive	Law	judge
Head of State	Oval Office	Opinion

Branches of the United States Government		
Legislative Branch	**Executive Branch**	**Judicial Branch**

Name:

Extended Activities for *Election Mania*

Bulletin Board Create a bulletin board display titled *In the News* with the following headings: *The President, The Congress, The Supreme Court*. Invite students to skim through news magazines and daily newspapers for photos and reports of our government at work. Suggest that students clip these photos and reports and post them on the bulletin board under the appropriate heading.

Interview to Find Out "How Many?" How many presidents have there been since you were born? Ask a grown-up to tell you about the presidents who have served during their lifetime.

Vote of the Day During math time, have a "Vote of the Day" by having students complete a simple questionnaire and record the results in the form of a graph. For example, "Vote for your favorite sport: baseball, basketball, kickball." Assign one child to be in charge of ballots and the voter's list while others count and tally ballots. Each day different groups can pose the question of the day and tally the results. The class could also vote on topics such as where the class should go on a field trip or the choice of a classroom mascot.

Conduct a Class Poll Discuss the definition of a poll as "asking a few people their opinion on a topic and then predicting the responses of many people based on the results of this poll." For example, ask students to name their favorite color. Use the findings to determine the most popular colors. Based on your poll, what color do you believe would be the most popular with all students at our school? Why? Ask "Why do presidential candidates use polls? How is this information helpful?"

Class Constitution - Discuss why rules are needed at home, on the playground, on buses, and in schools. Using this information, write a class constitution outlining the rights and responsibilities of the students. After the constitution has been written in final form and approved by a class vote, have each student sign his/her name to signify approval.

Nations of the World - Using *The World Almanac*, have cooperative learning groups search through the section "Nations of the World" to find and locate the different types of government. It is an interesting assortment from Federal Republic (United States) to Constitutional Monarchy. The words are difficult, but children can learn how to locate the specific information. While doing it, they will learn that there are many nations of the world and many different types of governments.

You Be the Judge - Invite students to make craft-stick puppets of judges. Then ask students to recall the story of "The Three Bears" and to list the things Goldilocks did. (She went into the bear's house uninvited, she ate their food, she broke a chair, she slept in a bear's bed, and she ran away when the bears found her.) Invite the students to work in small groups to create finger plays in which they judge Goldilocks' actions. Have them decide whether they think Goldilocks broke any laws. Have each group share their decision.

Resources for *Election Mania*

Baicker, Karen. *The Election Activity Book: Dozens of Activities that Help Kids Learn about Voting, Campaigns, Our Government.* Scholastic Teaching Resources, 2012. Help students understand the election process with these quick, easy, and engaging activities that teach about how we elect our leaders; the presidency; the rights and responsibilities of voting; the differences between local, state, and national government. It includes a write & read mini-book, election time line, polling and graphing activities, updated and revised literature links and Web site connections.

Barnes, Peter W. and Cheryl Shaw. *House Mouse, Senate Mouse*. Little Patriot Press, 2012. This informational storybook tells about how our laws are made at the nations' Capitol. Part of the "Mice" book series that teaches about the institutions of the United States Government, this fanciful tale has the Squeaker of the House and the Senate Mouse-jority debating a law to declare a National Cheese proposed by Miss Tuftmouse's second grade class. It takes students through the legislative process, from the basic research of a bill, through committee consideration and to signing at the President's desk.

Barnes, Peter W. and Cheryl Shaw. *House Mouse, Senate Mouse*. Alexandria, Virginia: VSP Books. 1996. ISBN 0-9637688-4-0. This informational storybook tells about how our laws are made at the nations' capitol. This fanciful tale has the Squeaker of the House and the Senate Mouse-jority debating a law to declare a National Cheese proposed by Miss Tuftmouse's second grade class. It takes students through the legislative process, from the basic research of a bill, through committee consideration and to signing by the President.

Barnes, Peter W. and Cheryl Shaw. *Marshall, the Courthouse Mouse*. Little Patriot Press, 2012. This informational storybook tells about our nation's judicial system and the Supreme Court. Part of the "Mice" book series that teaches about the institutions of the United States Government, this fanciful tale has Marshall J. Mouse, the Chief Justice of the Supreme Court of the United Mice of America, lead his fellow justices in deciding whether to uphold a law requiring all mice to eat the same cheese on certain days, or to strike the law down, giving the mice the freedom to eat any cheese they want, any time.

Barnes, Peter W. and Cheryl Shaw. *Woodrow, the White House Mouse*. Little Patriot Press, 2012. Every four years, like the rest of us do, the mice of the nation elect someone too. This informational storybook tells about the presidency and the nation's most famous house, the White House. Part of the "Mice" book series that teaches about the institutions of the United States Government, this fanciful tale has the United Mice of America elect Woodrow G. Washingtail as their president.

Branches of Government, Set of 3 Posters. Item # 7008P. Knowledge Unlimited. Displayed together, these three posters help students compare the executive, legislative, and judicial branches of government. Displays show the qualifications, terms of office, and basic duties of the president, members of Congress, and justices of the Supreme Court. 17"h X 11" w. Under $15. http://www.knowledgeunlimited.com/index.html. On the left side of the page, click on Posters. In the Search box, type in "Branches of Government."

Brown, Marc. *Arthur Meets the President*. An Arthur Adventure (Arthur Adventure Series). Little, Brown Books for Young Readers, 1992. Arthur is a proud American when he wins the essay content and is rewarded by reading it to the President in Washington D.C.

Buchanan, Shelly. *Our Government: The Three Branches* (Primary Source Readers). Teacher Created Materials, 2014. The nation's founders split the government into three branches. This ensured that no one person would have too much power. Colorful images, supporting text, a glossary, table of contents, and index all work together to help readers better understand the content.

Cronin, Doreen. *Duck for President*. Betsy Lewin, illustrator. Athenaeum Books for Young Readers, 2004. Here is a duck who began in a humble pond. He worked his way to farmer, to governor, and now, perhaps, to the highest office in the land. The text is funny for kids and adults.

Fradin, Dennis B. *Voting and Elections*. Children's Press (New True Book), 1985. ISBN 0516412744. In this photo-essay children will learn how voting and elections work.
Hample, Stuart. *Dear Mr. President*. New York: Workman Publishing1993. This little book contains letters written by children to President Clinton.

Historical Documents. Parchment replicas of some of America's most important documents, including the Declaration of Independence, Bill of Rights, and U.S. Constitution. Write for a free catalog to Historical Documents Company, 2555 Orthodox St., Philadelphia, PA 19137. Call 1- 888-700-7265, info@histdocs.com

Munro, Roxie. *The Inside-Outside Book of Washington D.C.* New York: Dutton Juvenile. 1987. ISBN 0525442987. Striking drawings illustrate the inside and outside of many buildings in Washington D.C. including the Supreme Court Building, The East Room and the White House, and the Senate Wing of the United States Capitol. Historic notes are provided on the back page for each of the buildings.

The World Almanac and Book of Facts. Mahwah: NJ. The almanac includes up-to-date information on a variety of topics such as the United States Government, including a list of Presidents, current cabinet members, Supreme Court Justices and members of Congress. Published annually in paperback format, the almanac is available at most bookstores.

Viorst, Judith. *If I Were in Charge of the World*. Aladdin, 1984. This classic book contains a collection of humorous poetry that young children can identify with. Written with humor and understanding, Judith Viorst's poems are certain to delight children and adults alike -- and be read again and again. Have students write poems using the copy change method for "If I Were in Charge of the World."

Lesson Organization for *Election Mania*

Lesson	Activities	Supplies Needed
Lesson 1: Rules and Laws	Activity #1 Who makes the rules? Activity # 2 Who makes the laws?	Copy of Handout #1.1 for use by teacher with document camera; thin point black pen For each student, a copy of Handout #1.2 and one for teacher
Lesson 2: Local Government	Activity # 1 Our City Activity # 2 Selecting a Local Government for our Classroom Activity # 3 City Government Description Cards Activity #4 The City Council forms the Government	For each student, a copy of Handout #2.1. In advance, research each city represented by the students; display a copy of city seal, city motto; poster size copy of the Council Manager chart on page 10; Sign-in sheet of registered voters for polling place; ballots; pencils; voting booths; voting box; *I Voted* stickers (optional) For each pair of students, a copy of Handout #2.2 A copy of Handout #2.3 for the City Clerk to post the Class Jobs
Optional Activity	Visit City Hall Chambers and/or have a City Council Guest Speaker	Arrange for City Council speaker/s
Lesson 3 Neighbor-hood Problem	Activity # 1 Simulation: A Neighborhood Problem (If possible, conduct this at your City Hall Council Chambers) Activity # 2 Service Learning Project	Copy of Handout # 3.1 for teacher and, for each student, a copy of Handout #3.1 and Handout #3.2. Copy for each group of Handout #3.1
Lesson 4 Levels of Govern-ment	Activity # 1 Levels of Government	For each group, a copy of Handout #4.1 and a sheet of 12" X 18" construction paper folded in thirds and each section labeled with a level of government; For each student, a copy of Handout #4.1 and a 12" X 18" sheet of construction paper; scissors, glue sticks
Lesson 5 The President	Activity # 1 Presidential Quiz Activity # 2 Qualifications of the President Activity # 3 Selecting a Class President Activity # 4 Class Election Activity # 5 Who is Qualified for the Presidency?	For each student, a copy of Handout #5.1 Sign-in sheet of registered voters for polling place; ballots; pencils; voting booths; voting box; *I Voted* stickers; bible for oath of office (optional); For each student, a sheet of paper to practice signature. For each student, a copy of Handout #5.2
Lesson 6 Sort the Branches	Activity # 1 Cut and Sort Optional Format for Step 3: a Layered FLIP Book	For each student, a copy of Handout #6.1; scissors; glue sticks. For each student, a copy of 2 sheets of paper assembled into a "layered book."

Correlation to the California History-Social Science Standards

California History-Social Science, Grade 3, Standard 4

Students understand the role of rules and laws in our daily lives, and the basic structure of the United States Government, in terms of:

1. Determine the reasons for rules, laws, and the U.S. Constitution; the role of citizenship in promoting rules and laws; and the consequences for people who violate rules and laws.

2. Discuss the importance of public virtue and the role of citizens, including how to participate in a classroom, community and in civic life

3. Understand the three branches of government, with an emphasis on local government.

California History-Social Science, Grade 4, Standard 5

Students understand the structures, functions, and powers of the local, state, and federal governments as described in the U.S. Constitution.

1. Discuss what the U.S. Constitution is and why it is important (i.e., a written document that defines the structure and purpose of the U.S. government and describes the shared powers of federal, state, and local governments).

2. Understand the purpose of the California Constitution, its key principles, and its relationship to the U.S. Constitution.

3. Describe the similarities (e.g., written documents, rule of law, consent of the governed, three separate branches) and differences (e.g., scope of jurisdiction, limits on government powers, use of the military) among federal, state, and local governments.

4. Explain the structures and functions of state governments, including the roles and responsibilities of their elected officials.

California History-Social Science, Grade 5, Standard 7

Students describe the people and events associated with the development of the U.S. Constitution and analyze the Constitution's significance as the foundation of the American republic.

4. Understand how the Constitution is designed to secure our liberty by both empowering and limiting central government and compare the powers granted to citizens, Congress, the president, and the Supreme Court with those reserved to the states.

Made in the USA
Monee, IL
17 September 2019